I Remember Still
A Kid's Guide To Seville, Spain

Photography By John D. Weigand
Poetry By Penelope Dyan

Bellissima Publishing, LLC
Jamul, California
www.bellissimapublishing.com

copyright © 2012 by Penny D. Weigand & John D. Weigand

All rights reserved. No part of this book may be reproduced or transmitted in any form or by any means, electronic or mechanical, including photocopying, recording, or by any other means, or by any information or storage retrieval system, without permission from the publisher.

ISBN 978-1-61477-034-3
First Edition

"Look! I'm going in there-- and with one stroke of my wand I'll lull vigilance to sleep, awake the transports of love, thwart the machinations of jealousy, confound base intrigue, and overcome every obstacle that confronts us."

-Figaro

From The Barber of Seville/The Marriage of Figaro by Piere Beaumarchais translated by John Woods

I Remember Still
Bellissima Publishing, LLC

Introduction

When the award winning author, attorney and former teacher Penelope Dyan thinks of Seville, Spain she thinks about Alfalfa in the old kids' movie "The Little Rascals" singing the song, "I'm The Barber of Seville." That said, Penelope Dyan and photographer extraordinaire, John D. Weigand, set out in Seville, Spain to find the barber of Seville. Sadly, they found no barber of that title; but they did see some things kids would really like to see and saw some things kids would really like to do in Seville, right after they consulted with a few traveling kids along the way. What kids like to do and see and what parents like to do and see, may be the same thing, or it may be something entirely different. The trick to traveling with kids is basically to keep them quiet, happy and interested and to not bore them with a lot of spoon-fed facts. The same thing goes for learning. That said, Dyan sees with the eyes of a child, and Weigand captures what she sees with the lens of his camera. Children can use this book as a starting point to learn about Seville. And they can also use all the other tools Dyan provides, such as her kids web shows on www.stop4fun.org or her music videos on YouTube, for free. However, this is only a starting point; and kids and parents need to explore further in their quest for information and knowledge, because all of these things are merely a beginning, not a means to an end.

I Remember Still
Bellissima Publishinga, LLC

I Remember Still
A Kid's Guide To Seville, Spain

Photography By John D. Weigand
Poetry By Penelope Dyan

I remember it still,
that place called Seville.
From the sewing box of the queen,*
to the park and trees of green,
to the water and the streets...*
to shops filled with toys and sweets.

* The Costurero de la Reina (the Queen's Sewing Box, was built at the end of the 19th Century. It was the guard's house of the San Telmo Palace and grounds, which is today known as the Maria Luisa park. It is said it was used as a place to sew by Mis Mercedes de Orleans, who became the wife of King Alfonso XII.

*"The city is as large as Seville or Cordova; its streets, I speak of the principal ones, are very wide and straight; some of these, and all the inferior ones, are half land and half water, and are navigated by canoes."
Hernando Cortes

I saw a long, long palace
that was and is very, very grand,
that graced the green
so beautiful to be seen
in this very special land.*

*This is Saint Telmo Palace. In the 19th century, the Montpensier family made it their residence. The main front (in the picture) is from the 18th century.

The Bacilica de la Macarena*
is in the north of central Seville,
The Virgin of Hope (La Macarena)
stands here still.
She was sculpted at the end of the
17th century (as you might well know.)
And this is a place where you
should most definitely go!

* On the northern tier of central Seville, the Basilica de la Macarena contains the most revered image in Seville, "The Virgin of Hope, " the Nuestra Señora de la Esperanza, that locals call La Macarena. The statue of La Macarena was sculpted Pedro Roldán.

Here is a colorful church
for your eyes to behold.
It is the Church of the Savior,*
AND it is also VERY, VERY old.

*The Collegiate Church of the Divine Savior, El Salvador, is a Roman Catholic Church located in the Plaza del Salvador of Seville. It has been restored and is quite beautiful.

This was once the garden of
Saint Telmo Palace.
It is now a place of fun and dreams
of kings, princesses, princes,
of dukes, duchesses and queens.*

*All of this area once was part of the Palace of San Telmo. It was donated to the city by the Duchess of Montpensier, Princess Maria Luisa Fernanda de Orleans, on June 19, 1893. The park was not incorporated into the city until the Latin American Exhibition of 1929 when the City Council hired the French engineer, Forestier, to remodel the park to make it the main focus of the exhibition. The park is now known as the Maria Luisa Park.

And then there came
that very magical hour,
when I saw the Golden Tower.
Yes, it WAS quite a thrill. . .
to see the Golden Tower of Seville!

*The Golden Tower, or the Torre Del Oro, dates back to the twelfth century Almohad period. It was originally part of the city walls. It now houses the Naval Museum of Seville.

Then we drove up
and over the ridge,
and we crossed
a very modern bridge.*

*Puente de la Barqueta Seville/ The Barqueta Bridge "the bridge of the Expo," connects the old historic center of Seville with the new technology park and was built for the '92 Expo.

And later I saw it!
It was like Venice, Italy, right here!*
My mother said, "Please, do TRY
to stay calm, my dear."
I was so excited, I nearly
jumped out of my skin!
Because I just couldn't wait
for ALL the fun to begin!

*Among the buildings of the Maria Luisa Park is Plaza of Spain, designed by Aníbal González, who was the head of the architectural project of the Latin American Exhibition of 1929. It is a huge square surrounded by a semi-circular pond and this in turn by a building with a tower at each end. It's style is based on the typical architecture of Seville, with use of brick and tile.

There was a very small burro,
and you could be pulled in his cart!
And this place had museums that
were chock FULL of art!

You could pedal a bicycle car
that was built especially for two!
Now that was something
I really WANTED to do!

But wait there was more!
You could hop inside
and you could row a boat!
In front of ALL of those museums
YOU could gently float!
It was just like floating
merrily down a stream.
And the best part was. . .
THIS was NOT a dream!*

* This is a reference to the classic children's song "Row, Row, Row Your Boat" which you should feel free to sing at this point in the book, in a round or singularly.

You could even tour this park,
in a buggy pulled by a horse.
(Now, I just had to do that,
of course, of course!)
I couldn't believe it, but it was true,
I could not decide just what to do!
And so, of course, I did it all!
and I must say I had a ball!
Yes, I remember well.
Yes, I remember it still,
Because I had a whole lot of fun
when I was in Seville!

The air soft as that of Seville in April, and so fragrant that it was delicious to breathe it.

CHRISTOPHER COLUMBUS

www.ingramcontent.com/pod-product-compliance
Ingram Content Group UK Ltd.
Pitfield, Milton Keynes, MK11 3LW, UK
UKHW060133240426
12048UKWH00002B/20